SIMPLE

PLEASURES

SIMPLE PLEASURES

Haiku from the Place Just Right

ELIZABETH GAUFFREAU

PAUL
STREAM
PRESS

Paul Stream Press, LLC
Nottingham, New Hampshire

Old Man of the Mountain Image: Detroit Publishing Co., Publisher. Old Man of the Mountain, Franconia Notch, White Mountains. Profile Mountain Franconia Notch New Hampshire White Mountains United States, None. [Between 1890 and 1901] Photograph. https://www.loc.gov/item/2016801421/.

Other Images: Author's Personal Collection

ISBN (print): 978-1-7359292-9-3
ISBN (ebook): 979-8-9907913-0-5
ISBN (PDF): 979-8-9907913-1-2

Library of Congress Control Number: 2024911467

Published by Paul Stream Press, Nottingham, NH

For information: contact@paulstreampress.com

https://paulstreampress.com

Dedicated to my husband,
whose heart is the place I call home.

CONTENTS

'Tis the gift to be simple, tis the gift to be free
'Tis the gift to come down where we ought to be,
And when we find ourselves in the place just right,
'Twill be in the valley of love and delight.

~Traditional Shaker Song, Joseph Brackett

dirt road adventure
washboard, slapping branches, ruts
GPS turned off

old apple orchard
unplowed fields, collapsing barns
we take the back roads

covered bridge vista
leads us to an unknown past
farmer hays his field

July high summer
fragrant new-mown hay
family farm survives

another meadow
another abandoned farm
still the blackbirds sing

marble streaked with age
cushion of moss underfoot
gentle summer rain

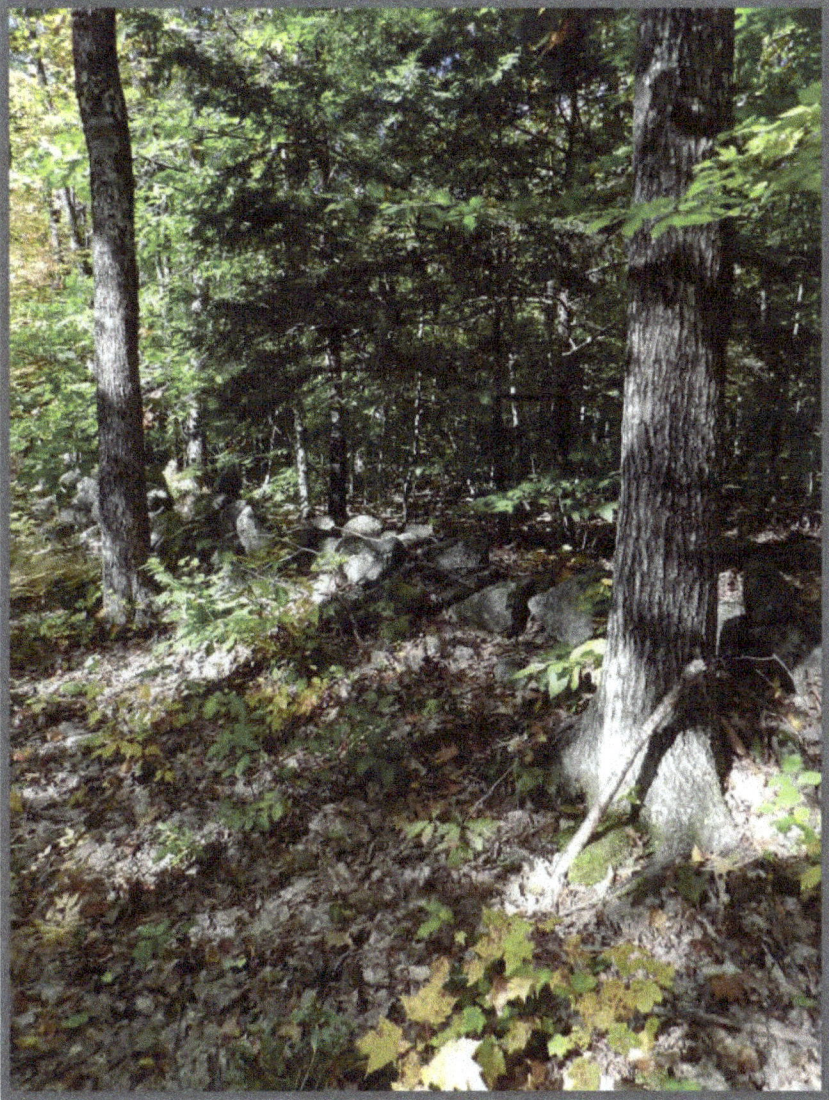

new-growth pines, maples
farmer's forgotten stone wall
a forest reclaimed

Old Man of the Mountain, 1901
(Image Credit: Library of Congress)

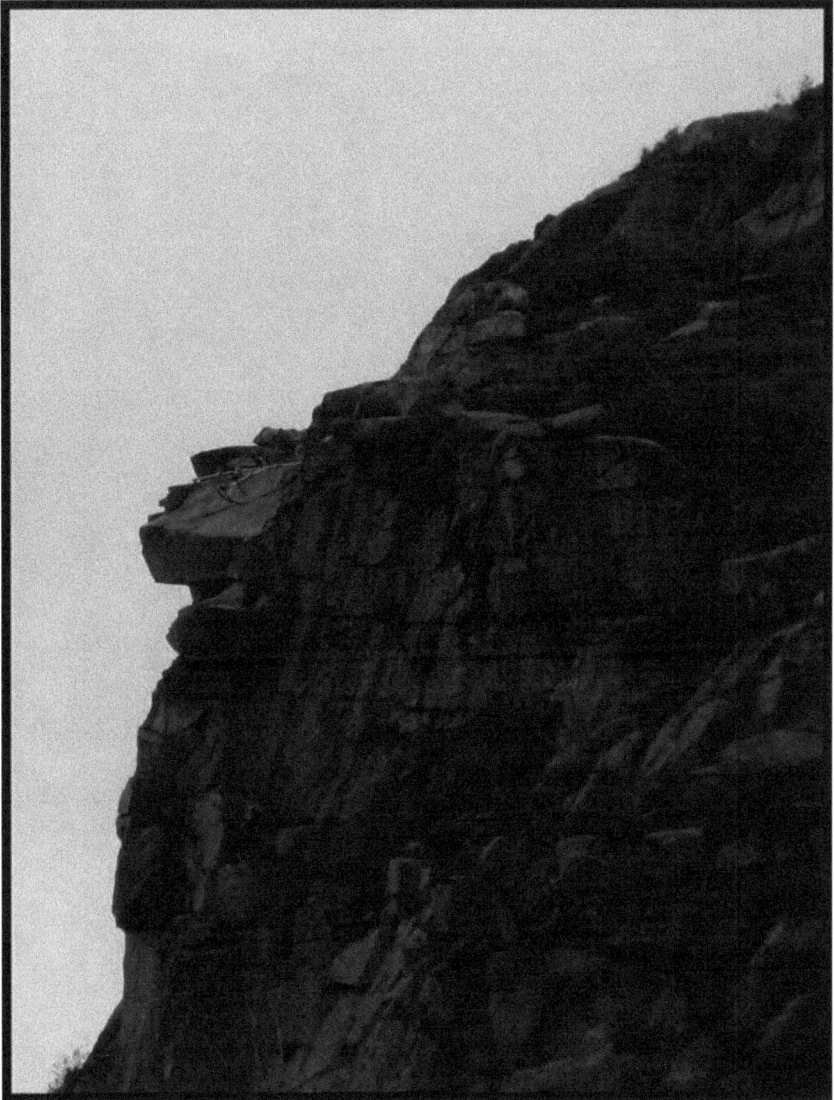

cables groan, strain, snap
Old Man of the Mountain falls
nature's law restored

back in the mountains
driving the Kancamagus
to a place just right

mountain air scrubbed clean
scent of early morning pine
unseen stream flows free

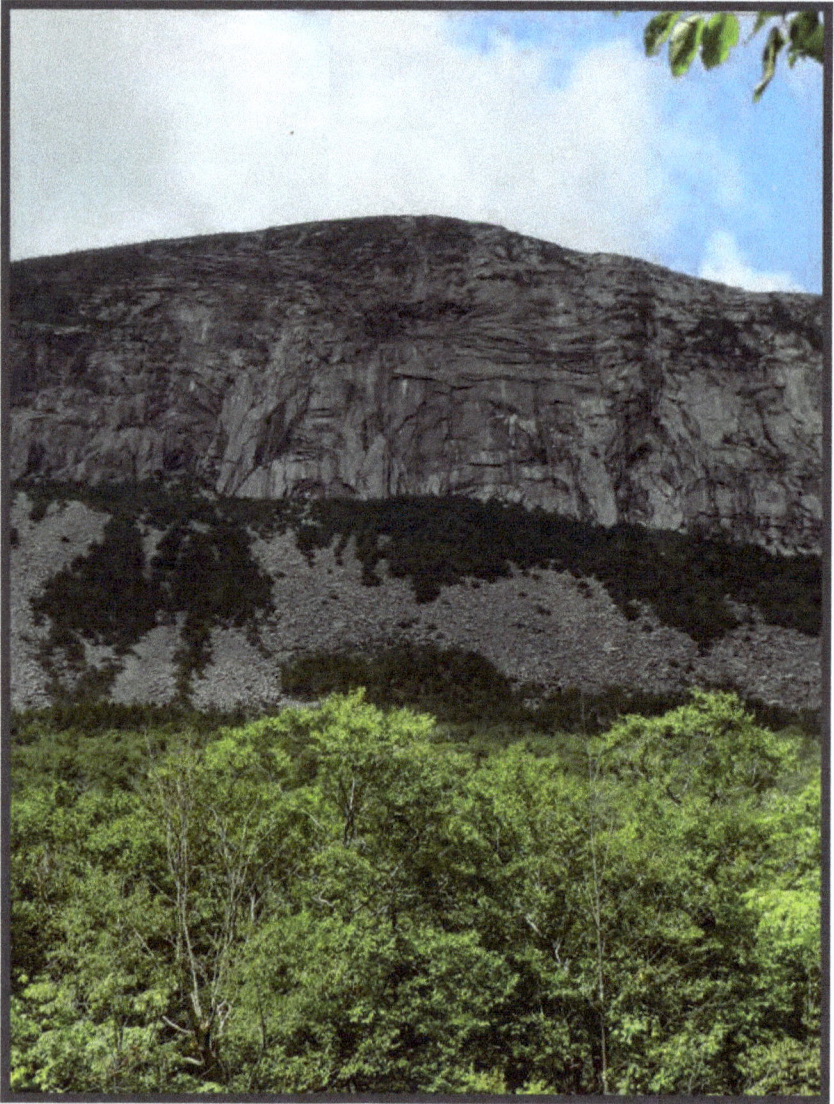

haphazard glacier
White Mountains crenelated
rock face left to climb

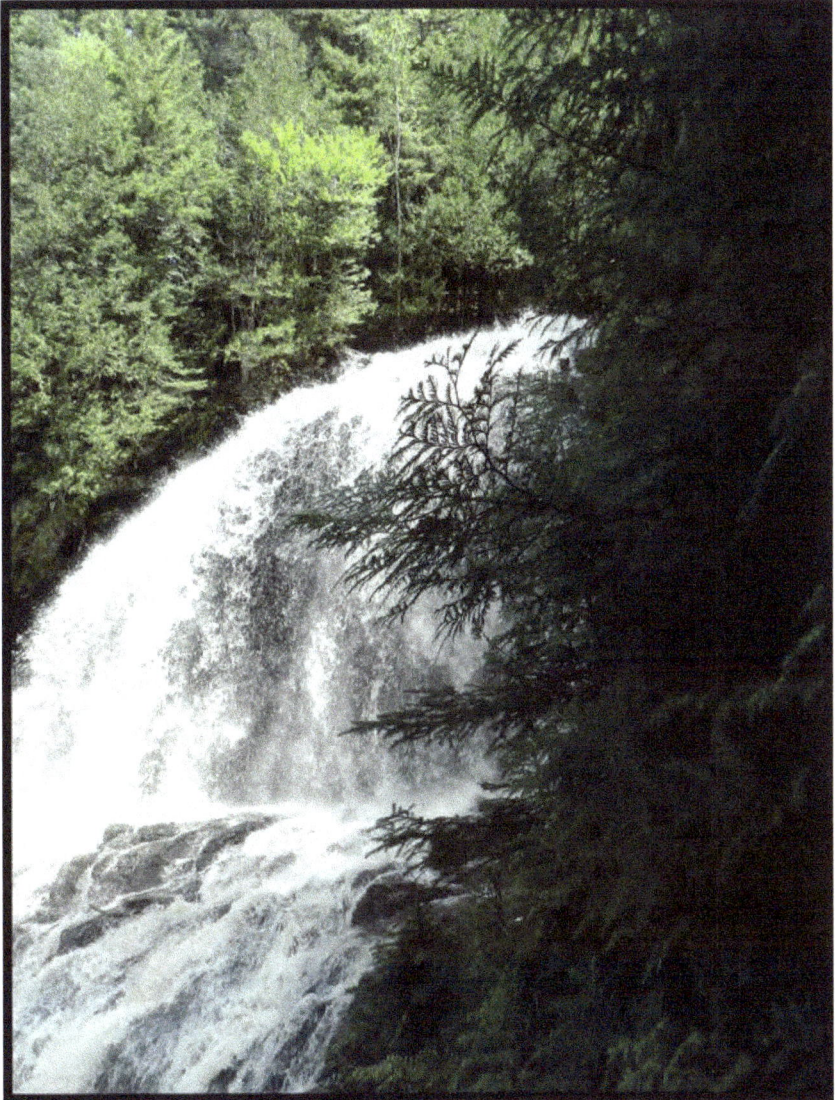

top of falls spindrift
we play rulers of the world
slippery path down

this sunlight through leaves
creator of dappled things
leaf mold adazzle

stand of white birches
roots entwined, canopy shared
indigenous trees

ombre sky, cool air
twilight comes to the mountain
a lone hawk circles, keens

back in the valley
a peeling fence to lean on
Green Mountains steadfast

clouds pass overhead
cast shadows on the mountain
roads close in winter

after the storm ends
calm returns to the valley
reverie in blue

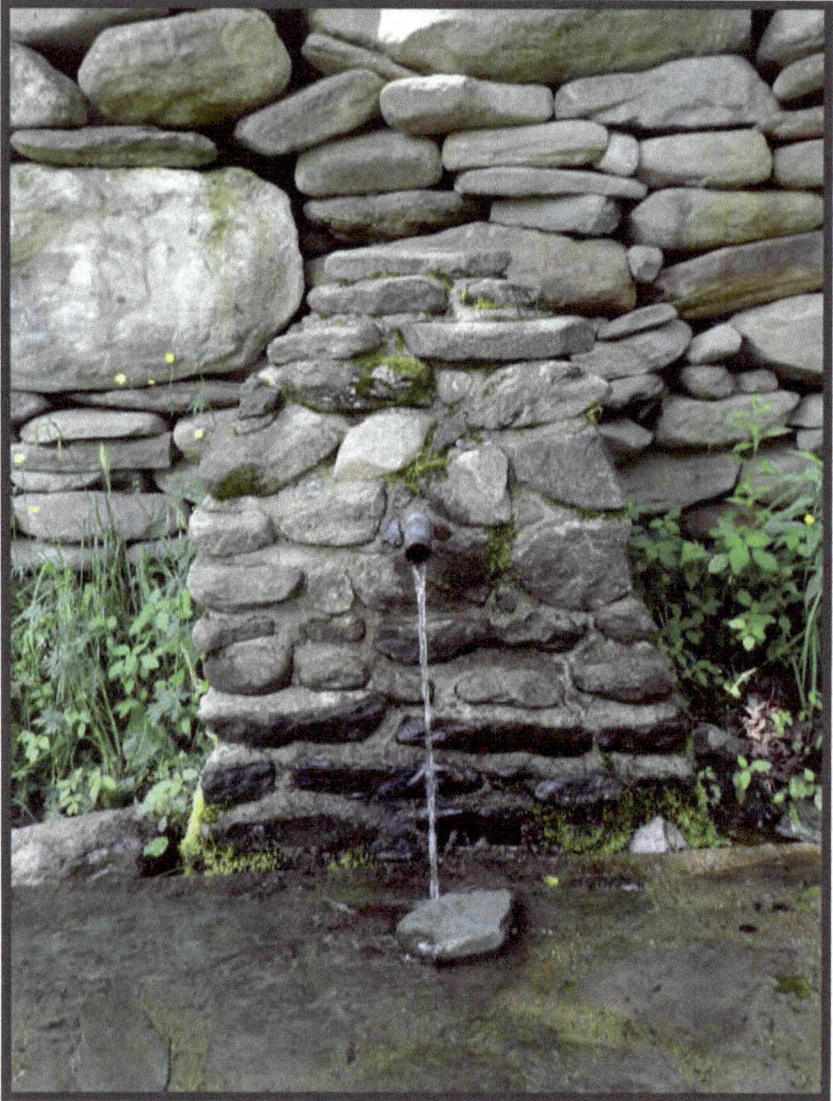

clear mountain water
rushes to a roadside spring
we stop, drink our fill

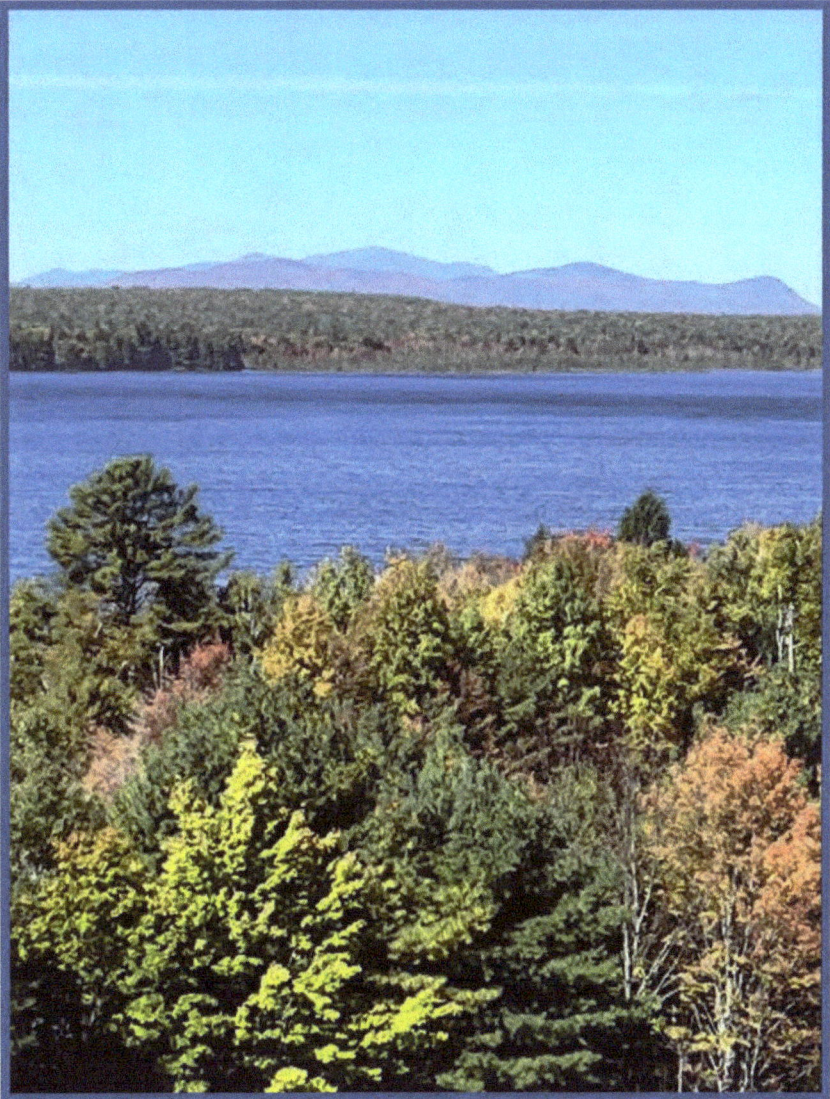

mountains meet water
saturated blue, faded sky
traffic rushes past

early morning sun
mist rises from the river
spiritus mundi

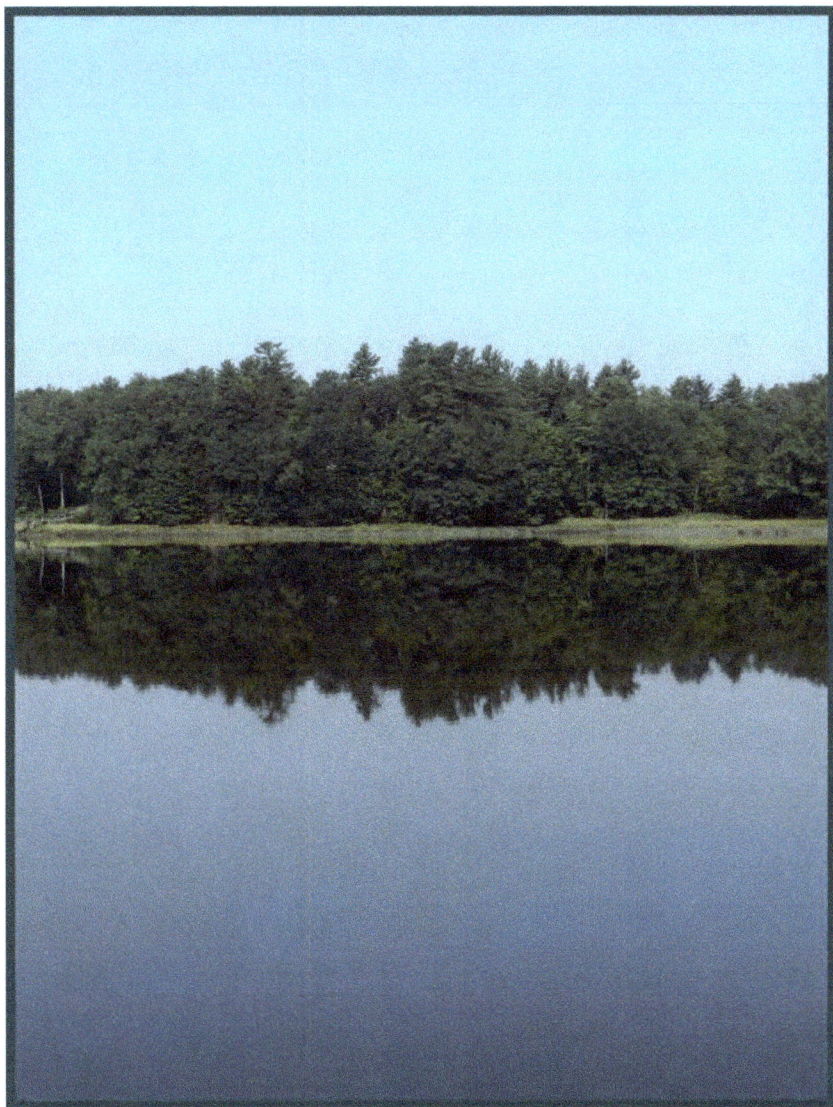

still morning water
reflected trees, cloudless sky
hint of tidal marsh

marshland lies quiet
grasses sway, water ripples
waiting for a crane

color trinity
sky, pine, striated ochre
ocean fog rolls in

gray heavens, gray sea
goldenrod out of context
lighthouse bears witness

Two Lights State Park, Cape Elizabeth, Maine

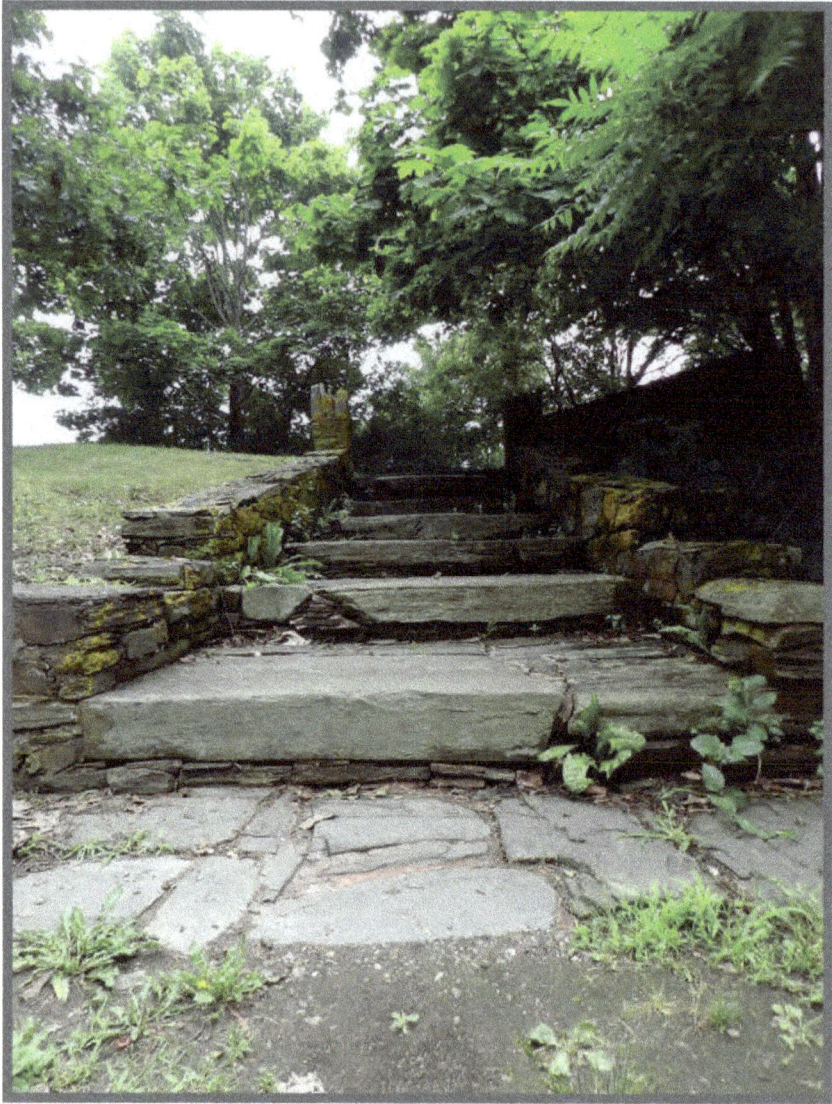

steps to the ocean
crumbling, overgrown, replaced
salted air unchanged

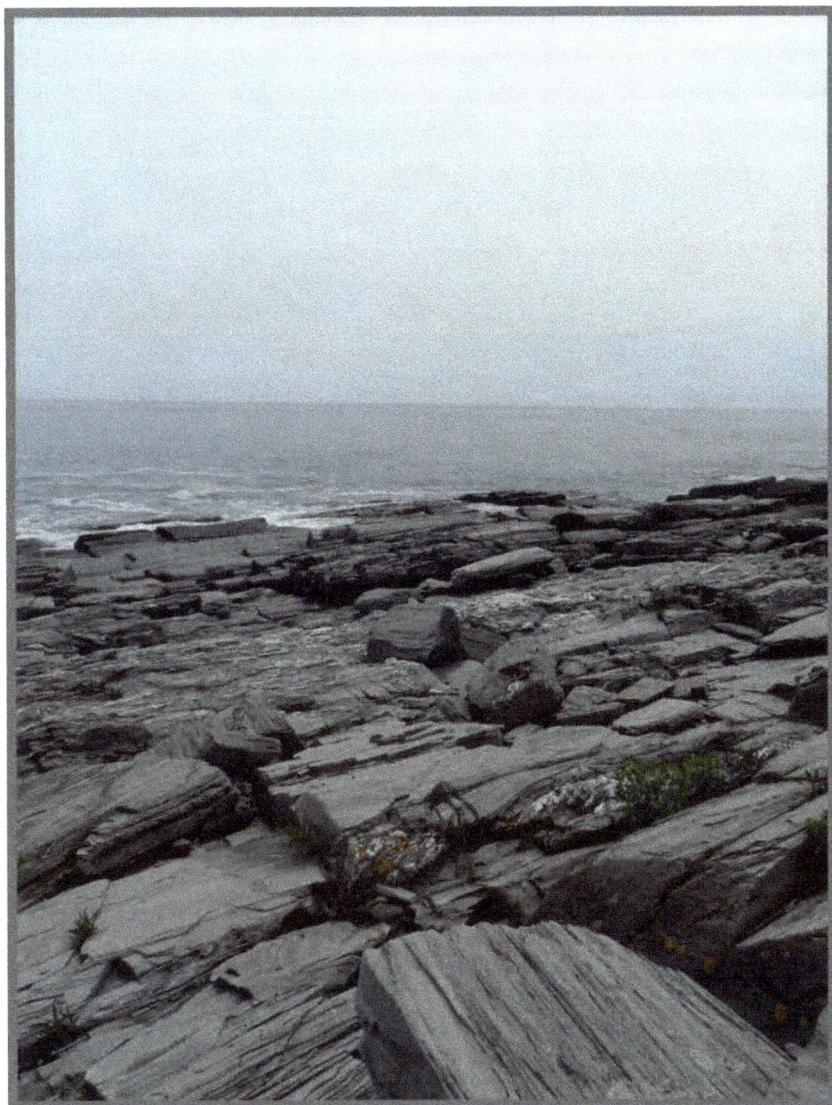

prehistoric rock
glacial detritus
unmoved by the tide

strong against the wind
rosehip jelly long ago
rugosa grow wild

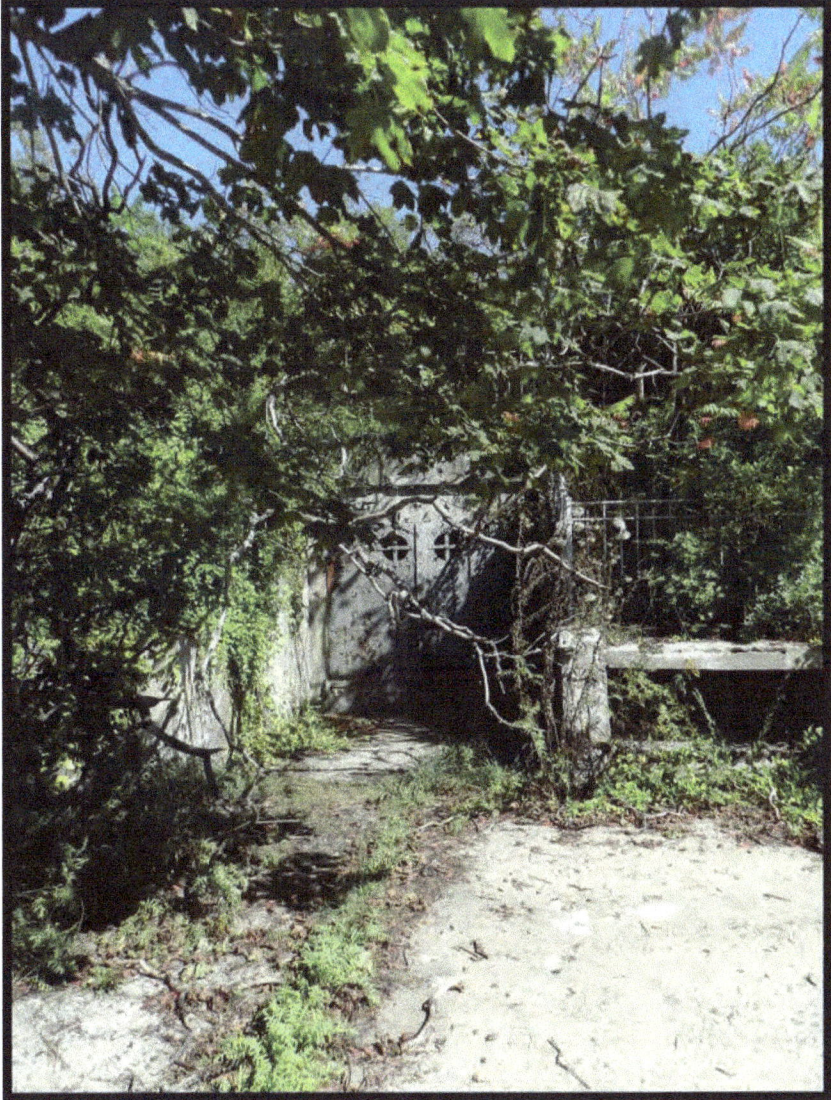

rusted bunker doors
overgrown with chokecherries
munitions no longer needed

rusted trestle bridge
calm water beneath flows on
riverbank adjusts

a shift in the air
scent of dying wildflowers
August cruelest month

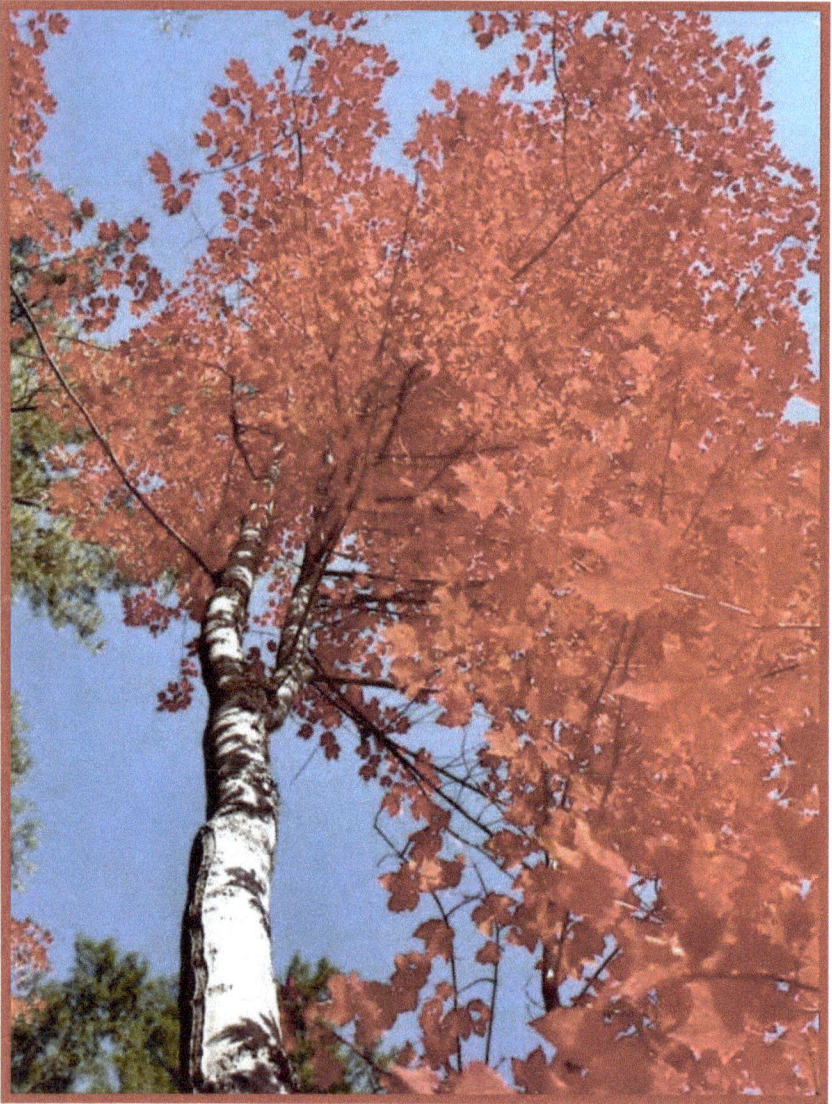

Jezebel maple
red, scarlet, vermillion
lives for the moment

capricious maple
what of this red, this yellow
in our own front yard

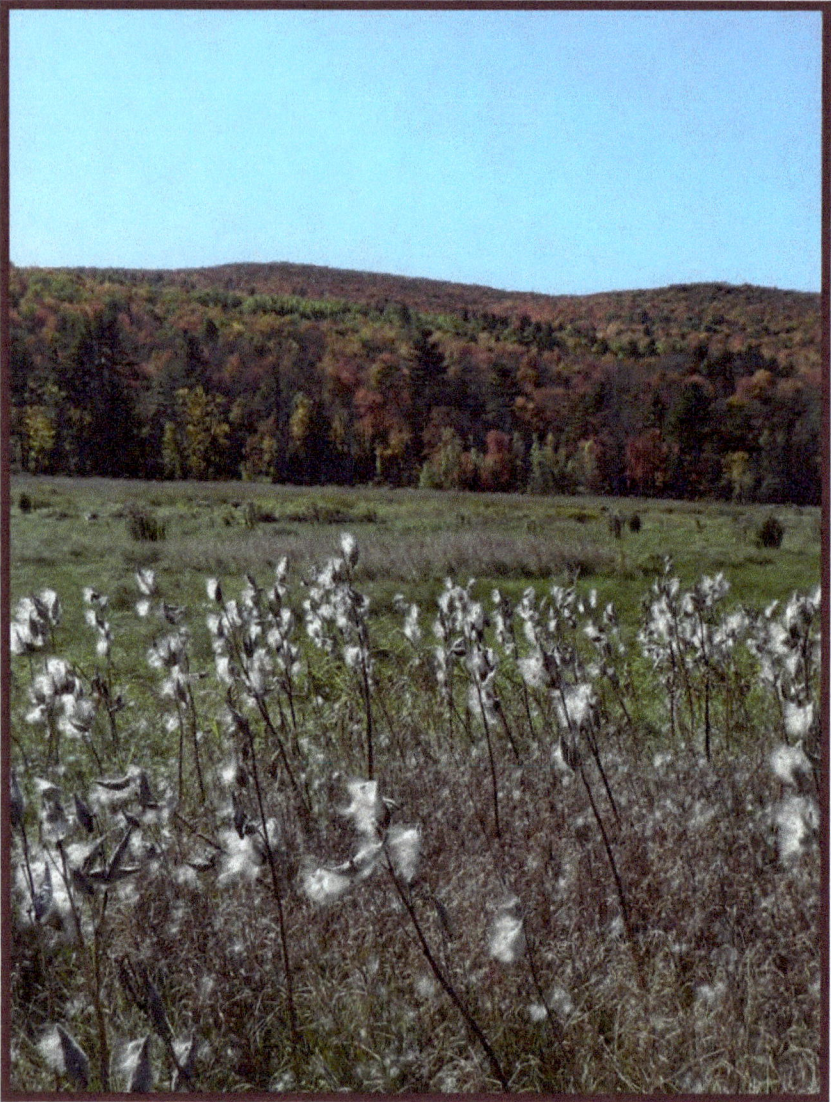

mountain foliage
milkweed open to the wind
monarchs on the wing

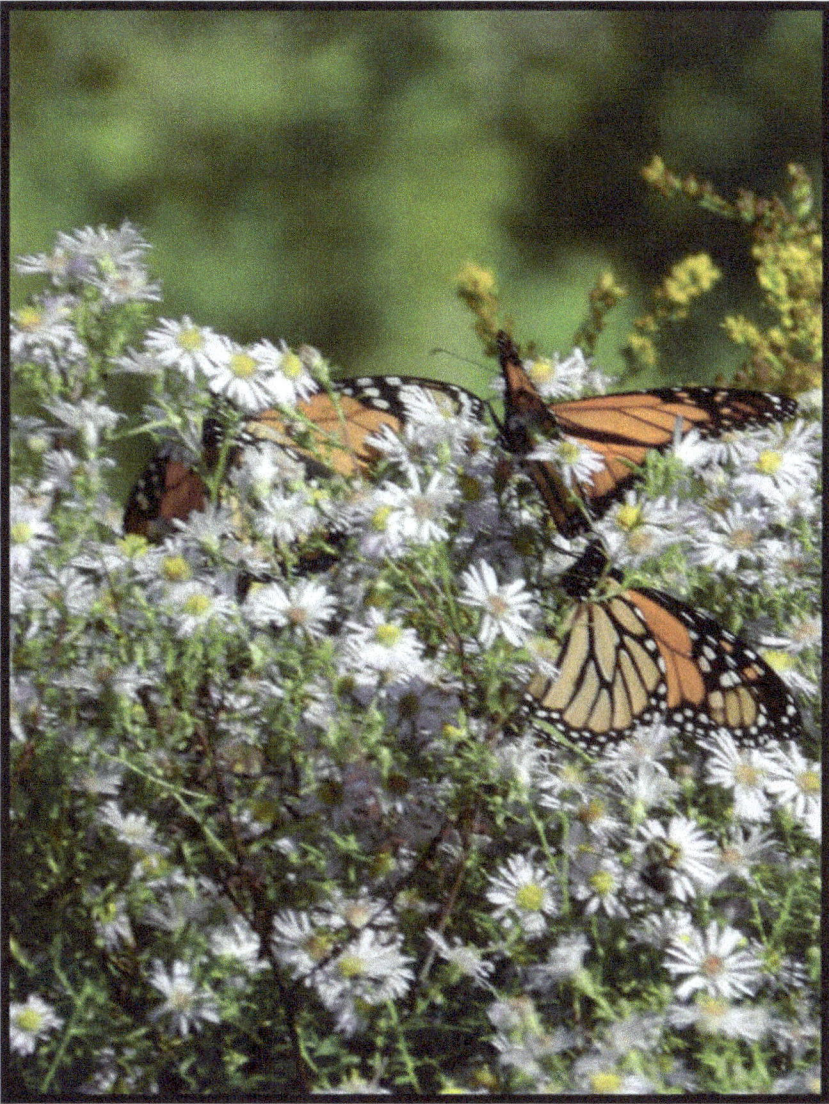

wonders of nature
my mother the eager guide
monarchs were the first

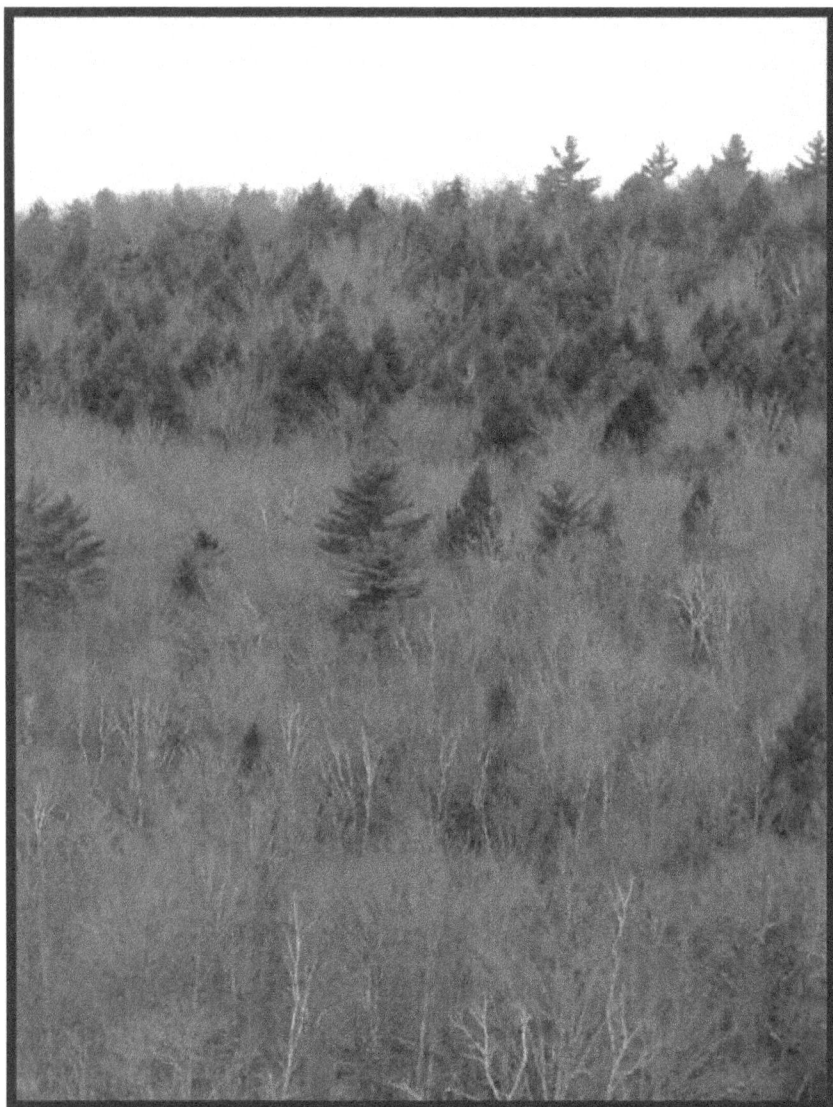

silver filigree
embroidered with evergreen
November remade

snow-laden trees, ice
driving the notch in winter
veiled in mountain fog

the pond in winter
windswept snow, crystalline sky
frigid air, silence

early spring snowstorm
lyricism all used up
oh—it snowed last night

river murky still
no view to speak of—and yet
our songbirds wing north

one more backroads drive
sap runs clear, maples bud red
spring begins anew

tree spreads its branches
classification unknown
we stop to marvel

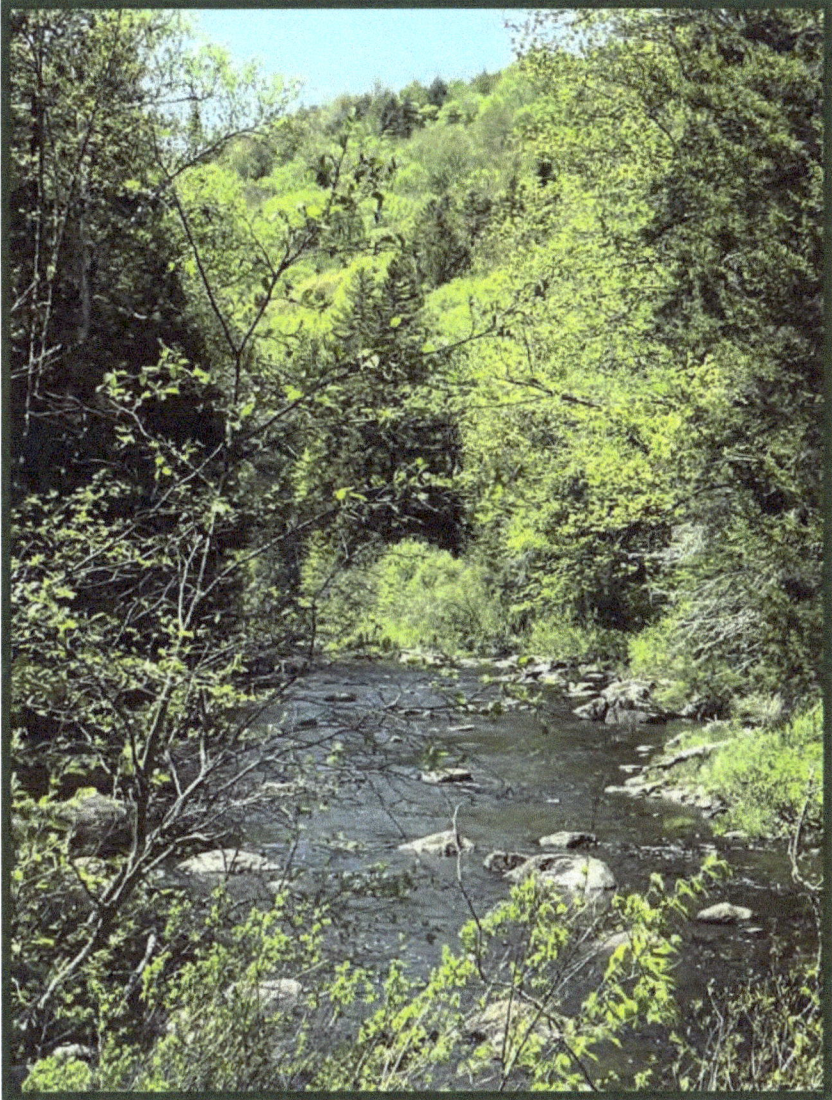

spring comes to Paul Stream
water replenished, leaves new
the past echoes still

landmark for the camp
wood splintered, lichened, missing
we cross with caution

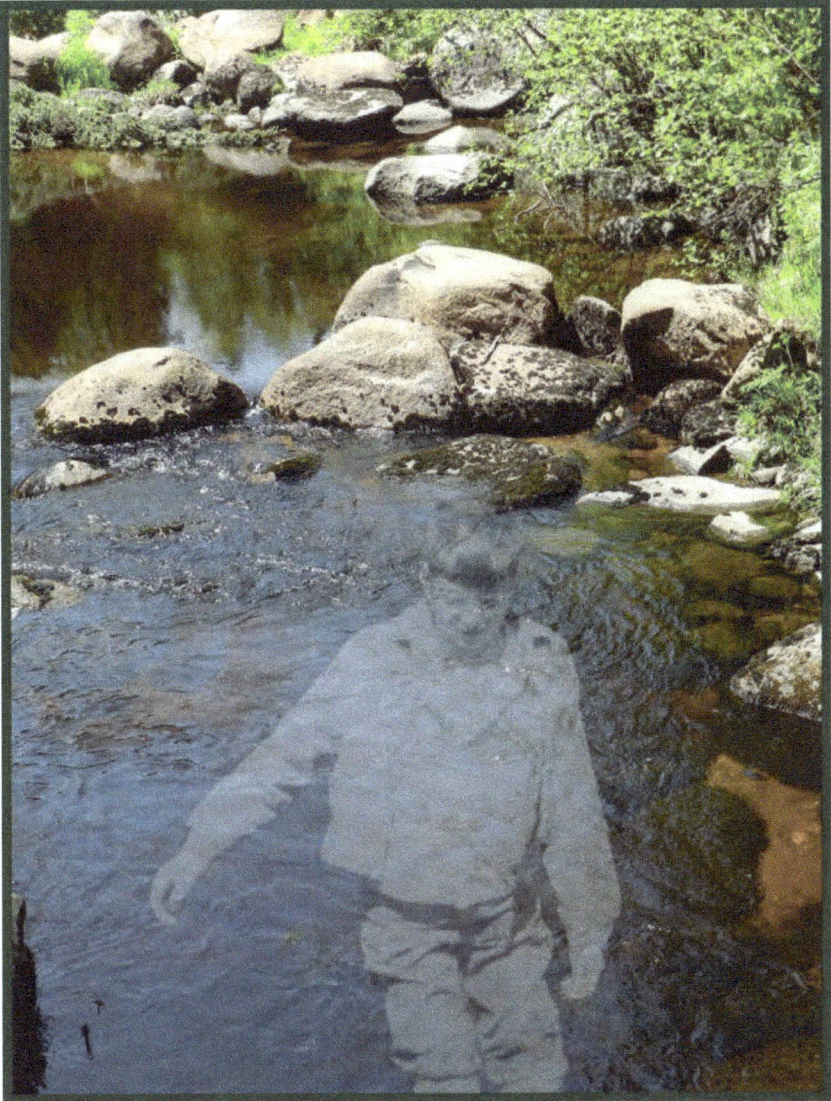

stream water eddies
swirling whirlpools, sun-warmed rock
our feet touch bottom

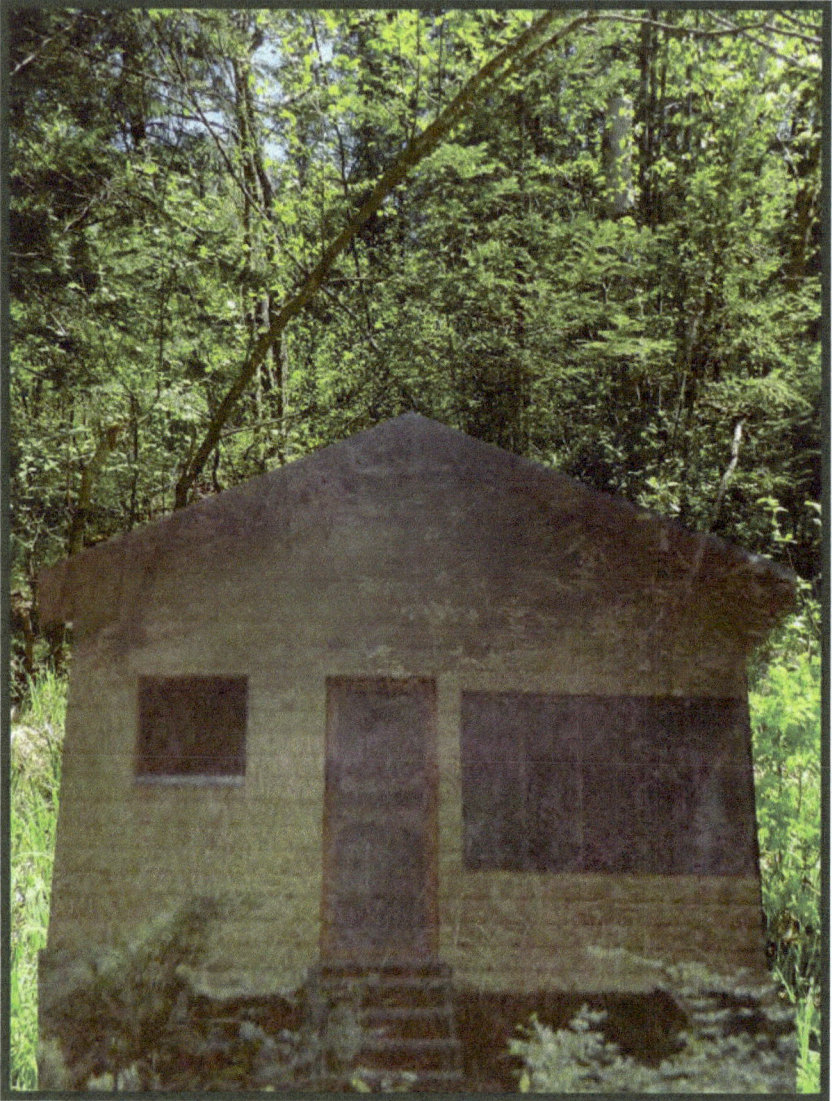

Paul Stream in summer
camp cot, book, open window
forest-scented rain

as if hand-tinted
the dawn outside our window
calms, comforts, transports

50

moon above branches
palest blue sky gilded pink
return home delayed

just an evening walk
the usual trees, grass, weeds
sky like no other

fading light, moonrise
day and night come together
our past, our future

mountain overlook
summer sun, marble in rows
final resting place

A Note from the Author

Thank you for reading *Simple Pleasures,* my homage to the sights, sounds, and scents of northern New England, my home.

The Inspiration for *Simple Pleasures*

My husband and I have long enjoyed exploring the back roads of Vermont and New Hampshire, as well as the seacoast of southern Maine. Some of these places are favorites from our growing-up years. Others are new to us, come upon by chance.

On one of these drives, the scene in front of me popped a haiku into my head. To be clear, I hadn't planned to write a book of haiku. In fact, I'd never written a single haiku, although I was familiar with the form.

I wrote down the serendipitous haiku and took a photograph of the scene that inspired it—then another and another and another until they came together into a collection. I have very fond childhood memories of the Shaker song "Simple Gifts," which gave me the subtitle: *Haiku from the Place Just Right.*

Thank You for Reading!

Again, thank you so much for reading *Simple Pleasures.* I hope you've enjoyed these glimpses of northern New England through my eyes and my heart.

You can find me online in various places (website, Amazon page, Substack etc.). https://linktr.ee/egauff Please feel free to get in touch. I'd love to hear from you!

Warmly,
Liz

ABOUT THE AUTHOR

ELIZABETH GAUFFREAU WRITES FICTION and poetry with a strong connection to family and place. Her work has been widely published in literary magazines, including *Coneflower Cafe, Soundings East, Hospital Drive, Blueline,* and *Woven Tale Press,* as well as several themed anthologies. Her short story "Henrietta's Saving Grace" was awarded the 2022 Ben Nyberg prize for fiction by Choeofpleirn Press.

Liz holds a B.A. in English/Writing from Old Dominion University and an M.A. in English/Fiction Writing from the University of New Hampshire. Her professional background is in nontraditional higher education, including academic advising, classroom and online teaching, curriculum development, and program administration. She received the Granite State College Distinguished Faculty Award for Excellence in Teaching in 2018.

Liz lives in Nottingham, New Hampshire with her husband.

ALSO BY ELIZABETH GAUFFREAU

Telling Sonny

Telling Sonny is a coming-of-age novel set in the 1920s, when much of vaudeville has devolved into the Small Time. Not so for Faby Gauthier, a naïve girl from the small village of Enosburg Falls, Vermont. For Faby, the annual vaudeville show that comes to the village is worthy of the Great White Way itself. Little does she know that in a few short months, she will learn the true meaning of Small Time, setting her life on a path she never imagined.

Readers Respond to *Telling Sonny*

"The last chapter left me surprised and more emotional than I expected. Gauffreau's first novel shows a deep level of story and character development, and I look forward to her next book."

" . . . Gauffreau brings us through the innocence of childhood to the mysteries of adulthood and all the feelings one encounters in a genuine awakening. In our #metoo point in history the story is a reminder of how class, sexuality and expectations were different. There is the underlying truth in this story that family matters and that community cannot be understated as important in our lives."

"I was completely immersed in Faby's story and was sad when I finished the book. That is the best compliment I can give to an author!"

"In Elizabeth Gauffreau's *Telling Sonny*, the strength of the characters is one of the irresistible aspects of this well-crafted novel. . . . I missed Faby when the story ended as if I were saying goodbye to a new friend. I look forward to Elizabeth Gauffreau's next book."

Grief Songs:
Poems of Love & Remembrance

When a loved one dies, the family will often turn to their photograph albums as an act of solace, to keep their loved one with them just a little while longer. *Grief Songs: Poems of Love & Remembrance* arose from that experience. The collection opens with three free verse expressions of raw grief, followed by a series of photographs from the author's family album, each paired with a poem written in tanka. Taken together, they tell the story of a loving family lost.

Readers Respond to Grief Songs

"Photographs and poems that tug at your heartstrings. Having lost a brother and both parents myself, this book touched me on a personal level. It is amazing how a few, carefully chosen words can reflect a lifetime. I have read it twice and found something new each time. I'm sure I will read it many times over. Thanks, Elizabeth Gauffreau for your words and images."

"This book of poetry is no more than a half-hour read, but what a lovely way to spend my time. Most of the poems are tankas, short syllabic forms of five lines, and Gauffreau is a master of this style. The collection is a beautiful tribute to the author's family and includes heart-wrenching, poignant, humorous, and sweet poems about childhood, family love, and loss. Grief is the thread that connects the poems together, sometimes overtly, but more frequently as a remembrance of treasured moments with people missing in Gauffreau's life."

"A family photo precedes each poem, and the combination of the two adds depth to both. Though the poems are intensely personal to the author, it was easy to relate to many of the experiences to my own family and the universal journey that families undertake. I jotted down my favorite titles and suddenly realized I had written down half the book. I highly recommend this short collection to readers who enjoy poetry that speaks to the heart."

Purchase *Telling Sonny*:
https://books2read.com/TellingSonny

Purchase *Grief Songs*:
https://books2read.com/GriefSongs

www.ingramcontent.com/pod-product-compliance
Lightning Source LLC
Chambersburg PA
CBHW051249020426
42333CB00025B/3121